D0975914

short cuts to happiness

ALSO BY TAL BEN-SHAHAR

The Joy of Leadership: How Positive Psychology Can Maximize Your Impact (and Make You Happier) in a Challenging World

Choose the Life You Want: The Mindful Way to Happiness

Happier: Learn the Secrets to Daily Joy and Lasting Fulfillment

Even Happier: A Gratitude Journal for Daily Joy and Lasting Fulfillment

Being Happy: You Don't Have to Be Perfect to Lead a Richer, Happier Life

short cuts to happiness

life-changing lessons from my barber

tal ben-shahar

THE EXPERIMENT
NEW YORK

Short Cuts to Happiness: *Life-Changing Lessons from My Barber*

Originally published in Israel as *שיחות עם הספר שלי* and in France as *Conversations avec mon coiffeur: pour aimer la vie* in 2017.

First published in North America by The Experiment, LLC, in 2018.

The Experiment, LLC | 220 East 23rd Street, Suite 600 | New York, NY 10010-4658
theexperimentpublishing.com

Library of Congress Cataloging-in-Publication Data

Names: Ben-Shahar, Tal, author.
Title: Short cuts to happiness : life-changing lessons from my barber / Tal Ben-Shahar.
Other titles: Sihot im ha-sapar sheli. English
Description: New York : Experiment, 2018. | Description based on print version record and CIP data provided by publisher; resource not viewed.
Identifiers: LCCN 2018009575 (print) | LCCN 2018013049 (ebook) | ISBN 9781615195121 (Ebook) | ISBN 9781615194872 (cloth)
Subjects: LCSH: Happiness.
Classification: LCC BF575.H27 (ebook) | LCC BF575.H27 B44613 2018 (print) | DDC 158--dc23

LC record available at https://lccn.loc.gov/2018009575
ISBN 978-1-61519-487-2
Ebook ISBN 978-1-61519-512-1

Cover and text design by Sarah Smith
Back flap author photograph by Judy Rand
Back cover photograph by Naomi Redel

Manufactured in the United States of America

First printing September 2018
10 9 8 7 6 5 4 3 2 1

To all the barbers and hairdressers
Who make us more beautiful
Within and without

CONTENTS

short cuts to happiness

INTRODUCTION

We go to the hair salon or barbershop in search of some kind of change. We ask for anything from a minor trim to a major cut, a barely perceptible highlight to a transformational new color. Many of us, however, secretly or openly desire to go beyond external change, beyond altering the way our head looks from the outside. What we truly seek is internal change–anything from a trim to a transformation of that which goes on inside our head.

As a result, many of us tend to have a special relationship with our hairdresser or barber. We freely share our cares and concerns, our sorrows and secrets, as we seamlessly extend the trust we have in their adept hands, swinging sharp scissors, to an overall trust in them. And when our defenses are down, when resistance is gone, when the wall separating us from the world collapses, it is then that we are ready to listen, to grow, to learn.

This book is about the big lessons I learned from my barber, Avi Peretz, who for almost twenty years has been working in the same small salon in a small neighborhood in Ramat Hasharon, a small suburb of Tel Aviv. The salon is a well-known fixture in the local landscape, located in the neighborhood center, alongside Café Caramel, Yuval's convenience store, and Jacob's grocer. Together, these entities encircle an area paved with large tiles, unevenly spread, some of them broken; a wooden bench that was once green, now worn out by the harsh Mediterranean sun; and a few dozen postboxes, each belonging to a family living nearby. Witnessing this all is the old tree with roots bulging out of the paved floor, providing shade to the grown-ups talking about their new startup, the children playing tag, the cats and dogs and pigeons coexisting peacefully.

In the midst of all this, Avi's salon is a gathering place that provides women, men, and children living in the neighborhood much more than a hairdo. His relaxed manner and generous hospitality, his wit and wisdom, affords people just what the fast-paced, high-tech, postmodern world lacks.

* * *

I had been going to Avi for a haircut since 2010, shortly after returning to Israel from the United States. And though I always enjoyed my time in the salon, and always learned something from Avi, it was only in 2014 that I started to take notes, to document the lessons I learned each time I visited.

It was ten years earlier, almost to the day, that I submitted my doctoral dissertation. Whether this was a coincidence or a carefully orchestrated move by my subconscious I don't know, but the point is that since 2004 when I completed my academic training, I had a persistent desire to return to school, to learn in a formal setting again as I had done for most of my life. And while I continued to read extensively after graduating, I missed the face-to-face learning I had been accustomed to as a student in a classroom. Starting to write this book was my formal return to informal education–only instead of a classroom I attended the salon; instead of a professor there was my barber. The lectures were short rather than long, with silence creating space around the words–words that were inspiring and thought-provoking, that communicated little theory and much practical wisdom.

In the following pages I try to convey the spirit and substance of Avi's teachings as I encountered them. Toward that end, the chapter progression is chronological, which means that some topics are addressed more than once at different points throughout the two years. Were I writing a traditional book or offering a traditional course, these chapters would have appeared in close proximity to one another, but I felt that going the traditional route would have taken away from the spirit of Avi's teaching–a spirit that is organic, natural, free of constraints, aligned with the way life unfolds.

I recommend that, to make the most of this book, you take your time reading each chapter and, after reaching the end of the chapter, spend a few minutes doing nothing, reflecting in silence, letting the ideas sink in. After you're done reading the book, you can leave it by your bedside or on your desk, and then every day dedicate a few minutes to reading a single chapter and applying its insights throughout the day. You can read through the chapters in sequence, starting at the beginning; you can pick your daily chapter by browsing the table of contents; or you can randomly open these pages, book an appointment with fate, and maybe discover a short cut to happiness.

on beginnings and what really matters

It was March 14, 2014. I was going through a particularly difficult period, drowning myself in existential angst over the "big picture" questions. I had just finished teaching an intensive yearlong program in positive psychology, and felt the emptiness that often follows an emotional high. What should I do next? What do I want to do with the rest of my life? Am I making a real difference? Does any of it matter?

And, to make things worse, I was about to board a long flight to China to deliver another lecture, and I couldn't help but think of Sisyphus who has just reached the peak, only to be summoned to the foot of the mountain once more, to go through the motion, once again, and again, and again.

I also desperately needed a haircut, so a couple of hours before I had to leave for the airport I went to my barber, Avi Peretz. As I was waiting on the sofa in his salon, I heard a female client ask Avi whether he had already received his pilot's license; Avi responded that he hadn't. When it was my turn, I couldn't help but inquire further.

"I didn't know you were working toward a pilot's license."

"Yes, I did it because I thought it would be the answer to the emptiness I experienced sometimes. There were, in fact, many other things that I thought would fill me up, but I realized that I was looking in the wrong places."

"So what does fill you up?"

"The little things that are right here." He pointed with his hand, the one without the scissors, to the ground where he was standing. "It's right here. Not up there, or out there."

"What are those little things for you?" I asked.

"Oh, it's the usual stuff. Spending time with my kids, listening to music, going to the beach." He then smiled and added, "Talking to my clients."

Being reminded of the value of the "usual stuff" shifted my focus from fretting over the big questions to appreciating the little answers, as I'd recommended countless times before and was in fact about to lecture on the following day. I felt much better leaving Avi's place than I had entering it, and it cost me only seventy shekels (plus I got a free haircut for it, too).

This was not the first time that Avi made me feel better, and I know that other clients of his have had similar experiences. I also know that I am not alone in receiving valuable, potentially life-changing advice through unexpected day-to-day conversations—with a barber or a taxi driver, with a gardener or the cashier at the local convenience store.

These words make a difference—and can make even more of a difference if we pay close attention to them—because they remind us of commonsense solutions to our universal human problems: the short cuts that are right in front of us, but that we often forget or neglect.

The French philosopher Voltaire once quipped that "common sense is not so common." Walking home after my haircut, I resolved to make Avi's common sense more common, so that I could refer back to it in times of need and so that others–who are not privileged to have him as their barber–could enjoy his wisdom.

on growing through hardship

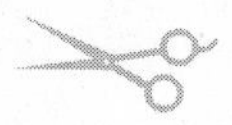

Avi grew up in Jaffa, one of the most ancient cities in Israel and the world. Because of its strategic location on the Mediterranean, overlooking the coastline to the north and the south, Jaffa was the site of much fighting as well as flourishing. Alexander the Great and Napoléon Bonaparte both chose Jaffa as a key strategic base during their battles over the region, though those battles happened centuries apart. And even centuries before those two conquerors landed, King David and his son King Solomon brought in trees through Jaffa's port for building the first temple.

Today, Jaffa is considered part of Tel Aviv and is a thriving metropolis–Jews and Arabs live together; ancient brick roads run alongside modern buildings. But when Avi was a child, Jaffa was a poor city, plagued by drugs and high crime rates.

Reminiscing on his childhood, Avi said that things weren't always easy–he remembered fighting, getting hurt, falling down–but that these experiences prepared him for life. "You see," he said, "if you've been there, to those tough places, and you come out, then you're less afraid of trying." I looked at his reflection through the mirror in front of us. His defiant, bronzed face seemed in perfect harmony with his words.

We talked about how our kids, living today in our peaceful neighborhood, were not getting the kind of real-life education that other kids got in the not-so-distant past. "Don't get me wrong," he said. "I'm glad my kids live in a safer place than the one I grew up in. The problem, however, is that we tend to overprotect our children. And there is value to hardship and struggle."

Harvard professor Clayton Christensen concurs, suggesting that challenges that children face when they're young serve an important purpose: "They help them hone and develop the capabilities they need to succeed throughout their lives.

Coping with a difficult teacher, failing at a sport, learning to navigate the complex social structure of cliques in school–all those things become courses in the school of experience."

Fortunately, life hands all of us some hardship. Even in the safest neighborhoods, in the most protected home environments, there are still opportunities for learning and development. And we, as parents, should not deprive our children–or ourselves–of these opportunities.

on highlights and insights

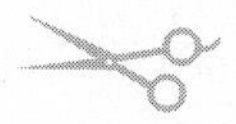

The next day I walked past the salon and through the window saw a few of my friends sitting on Avi's couch, a couple of them waiting for their appointments and the rest just hanging out there. I decided to join the mini neighborhood gathering. Given the small size of Avi's place–just over three hundred square feet–it was crowded and noisy even with only eight of us inside, and yet everyone seemed peaceful and calm. Conversations were going on simultaneously, with Avi quietly orchestrating the entire chorus–cutting hair while serving coffee, offering a smile or a nod of agreement.

Since we all send our kids to the same local elementary school, conversations often gravitate toward the latest drama unfolding in the classroom. This time, one of the fathers complained about his eleven-year-old daughter being left out of a WhatsApp group, and how hurt she was. Another mother said that considering what was talked about in her kids' WhatsApp groups (or, at least, what parts of the conversation she actually saw), she would have been glad if they had been left out. We went back and forth talking about how the simple act of talking has changed so much from when we were kids, and how much easier it is for children–and even adults–to be rude to each other thanks to social media.

Avi had until then been quiet, precisely folding squares of silver-foil highlights over strands of one mother's hair. I wasn't sure whether he was listening to us, until he broke his silence: "I told my kids that each time they hurt someone, whether virtually or face-to-face, they poison their body." He paused as he took hold of another chunk of hair for the foil, then added: "I tell them that I sometimes hurt other people and poison myself, too. But I'm always working on becoming a better person."

The commotion continued, each parent offering his or her own tips, but Avi's words stuck with me most. He'd said so much. First, he explained to his kids that when they put others down, they were paying a personal price–poisoning themselves. Avi had distilled into a single sentence a vivid depiction of our innate moral sense–a topic on which volumes of philosophical and psychological literature had been written, arguing that with the exception of psychopaths, we all pay a high emotional price when we hurt others. Second, Avi offered himself as a role model for his children–not a perfect and unattainable ideal, but a fallible human being who's aware of his own potential for development.

To become better, children need that kind of role model. Adults do, too.

on vacation

Every few days, Avi's salon would receive a new bouquet of flowers that filled the room with their scent and beauty.

"These are gorgeous," I said while admiring the latest delivery. "And they smell great." Their fragrance displaced some of the oppressive heat that signaled the beginning of summer.

"They're white lilies. I was planning on a trip to Thailand this summer, but I have too many family and business obligations right now and can't get away. So instead of going to Thailand, I brought a piece of Thailand to me. We don't always need to travel to enjoy the best vacation spots our world has to offer."

It suddenly dawned on me why I was spending so much time in Avi's salon: It made me feel like I was on vacation. A simple haircut appointment could transform into a sensual experience, similar to one we'd associate with being on a long break from our day-to-day reality in some exotic location. Joining the perfume of flowers, the smell of the freshly brewed coffee invites the clients to slowly sip and savor. The gentle scalp massage that accompanies the shampooing adds touch to the mix. In the background, bringing it all together, the ever-present sound of scissors tapping blends perfectly with the flow of conversation and rhythm of Latin music pulsing through the speakers.

But there was another reason for the feeling of vacation. The word *vacation*, in English, comes from the same root as the word *vacuum*, meaning empty space. In contrast, the Hebrew word for vacation is *hofesh*, which comes from the same root as the word *hipus*, which means to search. Combining the two roots from English and Hebrew, we see that a vacation can be a place that provides the necessary space to search. Avi's salon, though small, felt spacious, with only the bare necessities surrounding the flowers; it was a place from which I could launch my search.

On my way home, I picked up some flowers at Jacob's grocer. After my three kids were asleep, I put on an album of Agustín Barrios, whom Avi had introduced me to earlier, straightened out my room, and made myself a cup of Chinese tea. For a few precious moments, I brought a piece of the world to me. I was on vacation.

on touch

The next time I came to see Avi was with our youngest, Eliav, who needed some of his curls curbed. Avi was alone in his salon, sitting on the couch with an open book. "What are you reading?" I asked.

"This is a great book that one of my clients gave me. It's by a Greek barber, who writes about his years of experience working with people. Much of what he has to say resonates with me."

"Like what?" I was curious.

Avi went on to talk about how he could feel how rigid people were–psychologically, that is–when he was cutting their hair.

"Some clients, when I touch their head, move with me, almost ahead of me. Others, they need to be moved." Avi paused for a moment, and then with a soft smile added that even the hardheaded clients can be softened. "Gradually, as I work with their hair and move their head gently, they let go and receive my touch. But you know what's really interesting?"

"What?" I asked, while trying to figure out whether I was one of his hardheaded clients.

"Once their head becomes less stiff and they start to move with me, they open up in other ways. They become less physically rigid and more conversational. It's like their body has let go, and it tells their mind to follow along."

I thought about research by University of Miami professor Tiffany Field on the physical and psychological benefits of touch, whether in the form of a massage, a hug, or a gentle caress. Touch releases chemicals that reduce pain and induce calm. Oxytocin, the love hormone that makes us feel warm and fuzzy inside, is produced when we touch and are touched. I remembered my grandfather, who rolled the giant palm of his hand down our backs or arms every once in a while, telling us that he was spreading love on us.

Listening to the words of "Show Me Love" by Sam Feldt in the background, I thought about how the world would be a much better place with more touch. Unfortunately, though, as a culture, we are losing touch with touch, giving up on a major source of happiness that is, quite literally, at our fingertips. The nice thing about touch, when it's consensual of course, is that it's always a two-way exchange–when we touch, we are touched; when we give, we receive.

And we don't need to wait for our monthly haircut to share that magic touch.

on posture

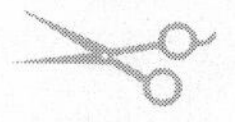

"Sit up straight." I heard the words of my third-grade teacher coming from Avi. But his words, unlike my teacher's words, which were a command, were more of an invitation. I accepted the invitation, straightened my back and elongated my neck, just as I do when I practice yoga. Sitting this way made me feel better right away.

When David, my eldest son, had had his hair cut a few weeks earlier, I'd watched as Avi ever so gently pulled his head upward and nudged his chin up slightly. From the side, my ten-year-old boy had resembled a proud warrior or king, a posture befitting his ancient name.

With my own spine newly aligned, I thought about research by psychologist Pablo Briñol on how our body posture affects our mental attitudes. For example, sitting down with our back erect and chest out can positively affect our self-confidence. Other research demonstrates how a slouched posture is both a cause and an effect of sadness, fatigue, and anxiety, whereas an upright stance makes us feel more positive and alert as well as less anxious.

Psychology follows physiology; the external and the internal are intimately related. A firm handshake communicates confidence and also generates confidence; a weak handshake communicates insecurity. The same applies to our facial expressions—a smile elicits pleasant feelings for the giver and receiver, whereas a frown generates sadness. The Buddhist monk Thich Nhat Hanh writes, "Sometimes your joy is the source of your smile, but sometimes your smile can be the source of your joy."

Avi always greets his clients with a smile, which usually earns him a smile in return. His handshake is always firm, communicating confidence and reassurance.

As I sit in my office right now, writing, I hear Avi's instructions to straighten my back, to lengthen my neck, to push my chin up ever so slightly.

on generosity

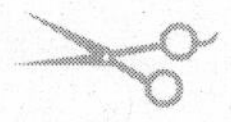

Avi was never into soccer, but in solidarity with his twelve-year-old son, who is one of the top players in our kids' school, Avi began watching the World Cup, taking place that year in Brazil. His vicarious interest in the game was enough for me to justify unloading my excitement over the match between Ghana and Germany (2–2 final score) when I walked in with my daughter, Shirelle: "Avi, did you watch the game yesterday? It was one of the best I've ever seen!"

"Yes, yes, Tal. A great game," he said, but he seemed to dismiss my enthusiasm more quickly than I would have liked. Moving on to more familiar and comfortable territory, he asked, "Would you like something to drink? Here, Shirelle, I brought these amazing granola cookies this morning from Erez Café; you must try them." Extending the buffet of hospitality, he pointed to a platter of fresh fruits on the counter: "Have some grapes, they're incredibly sweet."

As we were sitting on the couch, munching, the phone rang. I understood from Avi's end of the conversation that whoever had called was going through a difficult time. Before hanging up, Avi said, "Just stay by the café across from the roundabout. I have two clients waiting, and I'll come by as soon as I'm done." This was the middle of a busy day, but a friend was in need, which to Avi trumped everything else.

I have no doubt that Avi's charitable nature contributes significantly to his happiness. There is much neuroscientific research that shows how the happiness centers in our brain light up when we help other people. But the benefits of generosity go beyond happiness. A few weeks earlier, when Avi and I had been chatting about what it takes to succeed in business, he'd said to me that he believed that generosity was the secret to abundance—material and emotional. For Avi, unlike for French sociologist Émile Durkheim, there was no clear distinction between the mundane and the spiritual, the profane and the sacred, parts of our lives. He treated the words of a friend talking about personal issues with the same reverence as the prayers uttered in Darchei Noam, the reform synagogue in Ramat Hasharon that he attended during the high holidays.

Avi and I spoke about the root of the word *giving* in Hebrew, which is *natan*. This word is a palindrome, meaning it reads the same way from right to left and left to right. It's probably not a coincidence, as giving works both ways–when I give, I am given right back, and most of the time with interest.

As he was sharing his personal creed on generosity, for a moment I felt in the presence of a rabbi addressing his congregation, or a coach motivating his team. He concluded with, "Greed is expensive! If you are greedy, you usually end up with less–less material success and less friends."

Listening to Avi, I felt grateful to be part of his community, among his friends.

on losing our minds

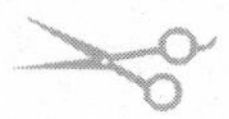

The busiest day for hair salons in Israel is usually the day before Rosh Hashanah, the Jewish New Year. Many Jews, Orthodox or not, like to have their hair done in preparation for the celebrations. I just didn't have time before the holiday that year, so I went for my haircut the day after Rosh Hashanah, and to my delight I found Avi alone in his kingdom. By avoiding the crazy-busy rush a few days earlier (because of my own crazy-busyness, I realize), I was gifted the rare luxury of having Avi all to myself.

It's also a rare luxury when a piece of music that I hear for the first time gives me goose bumps. But that morning, as I walked into the near-empty hair salon and heard Gnarls Barkley's "Crazy" playing overhead, my body reacted immediately.

When the song ended and I recovered my vocal abilities, I asked Avi where this magical song came from. "Oh, it's been around for years. But I hadn't heard this slow version until this morning and I immediately added it to my playlist. Amazing, isn't it?"

Since there was no one else in line, Avi suggested we listen to it once more before starting the haircut. So for five minutes we just listened to the slow, soul version of "Crazy," which transforms the process of losing our minds into a blissful escape:

When we lose our mind–our thinking brain–even temporarily, we make space for our soul, our emotions, to flourish. We experience the world directly, without interrupting thoughts. This is what Zen Buddhists refer to as a state of "no mind." It's about being in the world–not always, but sometimes–without deliberating over the past or the future, but spontaneously responding to whatever is in one's presence.

To enter this deep place of being and feeling isn't easy. We need to take our time, to slow down, to surrender to the present moment. We can do so as we observe our breath or look into our lover's eyes, as we leisurely walk outside or listen to a song for a second, third, fourth time.

And when the music ended, Avi took his time to work on my head, to catch me up with all the others whose hair was ready for the new year ahead.

on business

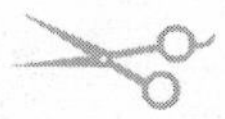

"I'm opening a new business," Avi declared to me one day. "I came across this new dye, and I'm going to import it here."

He pulled out his phone and showed me a YouTube video demonstrating a mild coloring product that could be used frequently without damaging the hair or scalp. "It doesn't contain all the chemicals that most hair dyes we have here do."

"Seems like it has real potential, Avi." Then I remembered: "You know, I just met the CEO of an internet marketing company who might be able to help you on the digital side as you're starting up. They use some of the advanced analytics tools that major search engines offer to identify the right market segment for different small businesses."

Avi paused for a couple of seconds before he looked at me and said, "Thank you, but actually, I was planning to take a different approach."

"What's that?"

"I know all about the power of social media and online networking. But I personally prefer the more . . . traditional way of doing business."

"What do you mean by 'traditional'?"

"I'm going to go directly to hair salons. They are the best places for getting to know and to understand the clients and their needs, whether they need my product or not."

It had been over ten years since I graduated from business school and heard a professor lecture on sales and marketing. But here was Avi, teaching me again.

"When I think about a business, I don't just think of the bottom line. It goes without saying that making a profit is important; however, it's not the only thing that matters to me. A good experience, for my customer and for me, is an essential part of a good deal."

Avi went on to explain that in neither business nor life as a whole was he keen on the impersonal data gained through mass analytics; nor was he interested in social networks that comprise virtual friendships and trivial "likes": "I want to gain deep knowledge through real relationships," he said. "That's how I've always run my salon, and that's why it feels like home to so many people." He gestured toward the couple sitting on the couch, enjoying the day's offering of grapes and peaches, as well as coffee.

Business today is associated with phrases like cutthroat or dog-eat-dog or swimming with the sharks or some other deadly metaphor. But as I watched Avi's expressions through the mirror, I vividly imagined him standing in front of a classroom, delivering an impassioned lecture on the importance of humanizing business. Why not substitute, or at least augment, impersonal statistics that reduce people to numbers with personal relationships that breathe life into a business? Why segment the market when we can use businesses to bring people together?

This approach is not only possible, but it could actually pay off in the numbers game, too. It turns out that real relationships, whether among employees or with customers, matter a great deal, not only emotionally but also materially. For example, research by the Gallup organization has shown that one of the best predictors of a business's success is deep friendships among coworkers. Today, these relationships are becoming more and more uncommon, and the price we pay—not just psychologically but also financially—is high.

In my mind's eye I saw a new sign on Avi's door: BUSINESS SCHOOL FOR THE SOUL.

on decision-making

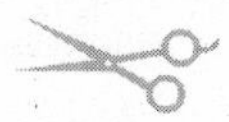

About a month after Avi told me about his new business venture importing hair dye, I popped in to ask how it was all going.

"It's going great. We're expecting the final OK from the health ministry to come in any day, and we have interviews lined up all week for salespeople."

"Wow, that was fast!"

"Yes, some things are going very fast, but other things are going much slower."

"Why? Is there a problem somewhere?"

Avi explained that he was taking his time on making some decisions, including how many employees to recruit, which salons to send them to first to start selling, even how many units to import with the first order. And then, generalizing from a particular instance to a general principle, as he often did, he said: "Moving fast is important, but so is knowing when to sit on the fence and wait." He then added, "It's not always easy to wait, and there is often a cost to it, but it's necessary."

Avi's words threw me back to Professor Joseph Badaracco's course at Harvard Business School, in which he talked about making tough "right versus right" decisions. These are the proverbial forks in the road, where following either path has merit. When faced with these decisions, we realize we cannot have it all–we must leave one path behind and forgo the potential value that would have come with it.

One of Badaracco's observations, derived from his research on great leaders, is that they often choose to wait, to sit on that metaphorical fence and endure the discomfort of uncertainty. This is precisely what Abraham Lincoln did before and during his presidency whenever he had to make a difficult decision, and this is what James Burke did as he navigated Johnson & Johnson through challenging times. Taking one's time is no foolproof prescription for revealing the path that is "more right" than the other, but sometimes greater clarity comes with time.

Avi concluded our conversation with: "The bottom line is that when it comes to some of the decisions I have to make, I just don't know. So I'm waiting, either to know and decide, or to know that I cannot afford to wait any longer and decide."

Socrates once remarked that he was the wisest man in Athens because he knew that he didn't know. Avi never said to me that he was the wisest person in Ramat Hasharon. He just doesn't know.

on lighthouses

A few weeks had gone by since I last saw Avi. I had been extremely busy, with trips to China, South Africa, and Spain—in addition to my regular teaching load of two semester-long courses when I was home. So at nine on Friday morning, when I finally found a morsel of time for a long-overdue haircut, I set out on the short walk from my home to the salon with a great degree of anticipation, excited about the new thoughts Avi's words would birth. By that time I was well aware of just how much I was getting out of my intellectual engagement with Avi's ideas. I often found myself thinking about what Avi would say in a particular client meeting or as I was responding to one of my students' questions.

I looked in through the window, and Avi greeted me with a smile. I smiled back and entered. The place was packed.

"Busy today, I see?"

"Yes, should be free by ten thirty, more or less."

"OK, I'll come back then," I said, feeling slightly dejected.

At ten thirty I returned and was greeted by the same smile. Karin, Avi's assistant, washed my hair and I sat down for the haircut.

"How about you try the new hair dye today?" Avi suggested.

"Hmm, I'd rather not," I responded. "I'm fine with my grays."

We talked a little about how his business importing hair dye was doing, that two dozen salons were already selling it across the country. I was impressed–clearly he'd made some decisions, and his waiting had paid off.

"But you know," he added, "even if the product takes off, I'm not leaving my salon. This is my lighthouse."

"Your lighthouse?" I asked.

"Yes, like for ships. No matter how chaotic or wild things get, this place is always there, lighting the way back to stable shore. We all need a lighthouse in our life."

Avi paused for a few seconds, and I pondered his words. "Do you mean the salon is your financial anchor?" I offered my mixed metaphor but at least stayed with the water theme.

"That too, but not only. I feel comfortable here, with the people and the conversations, the predictability of it all, the relative calm. And no matter how much I venture out and do different things, there is the lighthouse reminding me not to worry too much, that I can always get back to safety."

The twentieth-century psychoanalyst Donald W. Winnicott observed that children playing within a certain radius of their mothers display higher levels of creativity in their games than those who play farther away. This circle of creativity of sorts is a space in which children can take risks and try things out, fall down and stand up again, fail and succeed—because they feel secure and safe in the proximity of a person who loves them unconditionally.

I realized that as adults we too can create a circle of creativity if we have a lighthouse like Avi's—a beacon of safety and stability. These lighthouses can take different shapes and forms. For some, family or close friends make them feel secure; for others, the safety can emerge from a ritualized activity, like meditation or gardening; and then there are those for whom the reassuring light shines through the clean windows of a hair salon.

on laughter

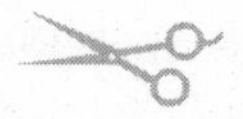

My wife ran into Avi in the neighborhood grocery store one day and told him that she'd been hearing about our conversations. "Yes, but we don't get enough time to really talk," he responded. When Tami told me about this exchange, I interpreted his words as an invitation to spend more time at the salon. So the following day I just walked in, short hair and all.

I must have come in right after Avi had finished telling a joke, as the woman on the sofa and the one whose hair he was cutting were both erupting in laughter. There was always a lot of laughter and talk in Avi's place, whether it was about the latest episode of *Eretz Nehederet* (Israel's equivalent of *Saturday Night Live*) or a personal anecdote that

Avi or one of the customers had shared. I stayed and listened for another thirty minutes or so, and as I got up to leave, I said good-bye to Avi and told him how much I enjoyed myself.

He said to me, "Yes, it was fun. I love coming to work, every day."

"What do you especially love about it?"

"It's simple," he stated. "I know that I'll meet friends and I know that I'll learn new things in conversation with them."

Aristotle pointed out that friendship and contemplation are the two pillars of a happy life. We are social animals and we are rational animals–we need friends, and we need to learn. Aristotle was so convinced of this truth that he founded a school of philosophy at the Lyceum, a place where people could cultivate friendships and learn new things at the same time.

I wonder whether they laughed as much in Aristotle's Lyceum as they do in Avi's salon.

on complimenting

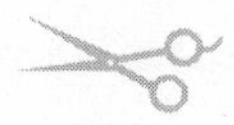

By now Eliav needed another haircut, so I took him with me. I was glad when I saw three people ahead of us–an excuse to wait and spend more time in Avi's presence.

The topic du jour was compliments. Avi was saying how some customers had been with him for years and yet had never complimented him: "I know that they like their haircut because they keep coming back." He paused for a few seconds before adding with a smirk, "Fortunately there are also customers who never shy from showering me with praise, and they make up for the silence of the others."

One of the women sitting toward the back of the salon, dark brown dye smeared all through her hair and on part of her forehead, chimed in with how she'd been married for over thirty years, and her husband never stopped complimenting her about how beautiful she was. "He knows that it pays off." She smiled mischievously, and for a moment looked like a flirtatious teenager.

Eliav was five years old and naturally did not understand what the woman was talking about, and yet he smiled. During the twenty minutes that we were there before his turn, he seemed transfixed by the back-and-forth, moving his eyes from one person to the next as they spoke. He felt comfortable, embraced, even though he was a bystander.

There is so much that is said and heard, disclosed and experienced, beyond the explicit words that pass among people. And children can grasp much of it, perhaps more than adults do.

"One of the perks of my work," added Avi, "is that not only do I get to make people more beautiful, but it's my job to tell them that they are beautiful. You too, little man," he said to Eliav, patting him on the head as he hopped onto the chair. The preeminent psychologist John Gottman explains that compliments are vital to flourishing relationships—between couples, among parents and their children, and in organizations. Compliments not only contribute to the relationship when things are going well, making good times better, they also make the relationship more resilient, better able to handle challenging times–which all relationships occasionally endure.

Mark Twain once remarked that he could live for two months on a good compliment. Perhaps that's why most people go for a haircut at least every other month–to be made to feel, and to be told they are, beautiful.

on love

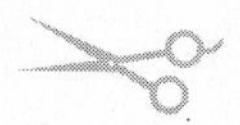

At the end of our previous meeting, I received a homework assignment from Avi: "Watch the film *What About Me?* It will blow your mind." I did watch it, and my mind was blown. The music was out of this world, or rather of this world–spanning five continents–and subtly underscored the various themes the movie explored.

The next time I saw Avi, I told him that I had completed my assignment and couldn't wait to talk to him about it. He smiled and said, "I love you, brother." I smiled back awkwardly and said good-bye.

There are very few people I've ever said "I love you" to, and they were all family members or girlfriends I'd been dating for months prior. But Avi told me he loved me, just like that. I knew I wasn't his only love, either, and wondered if he was cheapening the emotion by sharing it so freely. Until that day, I would have thought so, believing that declarations of love should be reserved for our most special relationships.

I'm no longer so sure. Perhaps Avi has it right, and I don't.

I had been reading Barbara L. Fredrickson's book *Love 2.0*, wherein she talks about a new definition of love as "positivity resonance." According to Fredrickson, we experience love each time we engage in a mutually positive connection with another person. Love, for example, can be felt when two people have sex, but it can also be experienced when friends warmly embrace, or when acquaintances look into each other's eyes in acknowledgment, or when strangers laugh together at a spectacle on the street.

Lowering the bar for the experience of love does not make it any less real or valuable. On the contrary: When we recognize all those moments for what they are, we appreciate them more and are more likely to seek them out. Love is all around us and can be present in each moment and encounter. So when Avi and I connected over the film—looked at each other, smiled at each other, acknowledged each other—that was indeed love.

I decided to make a point of saying "I love you" more often, when I actually felt it. Who was I to argue with Barbara L. Fredrickson, one of the world's leading experts on love?

on being part of the whole

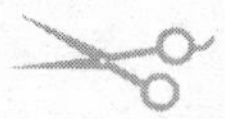

When I next came in to see Avi, I asked him why he had wanted me to watch the movie *What About Me?* He said that there were a number of powerful ideas in it, such as learning to live in the present rather than in the future, appreciating the beauty of our world, and so on.

"The key takeaway for me, though," he said, "was about shifting from self-focus to other-focus." He went on to explain how the movie demonstrates that we're all part of the same whole, that all of our actions are interconnected. "And if the world really is that way, if we are all part of the same mosaic, then it makes sense to broaden our usual narrow perspective and reach beyond the self."

"How do you mean?" I asked.

"I mean that if you reach out to others and contribute to their well-being, then given that you are connected to them, you are also contributing to yourself. If you just focus on yourself–me, me, me–then you're touching only a small part of the whole, and even if you do a great job of it, you are attaining only a tiny part of your potential for fulfillment."

Avi's argument made sense. After all, levels of depression were on the rise around the world, and one of the causes of this trend that psychologists pointed to was that people were becoming more self-centered.

"But focusing on yourself is important, too. If you don't give to yourself, you'll have nothing left to share," I added.

"Yes, of course. I am also part of that mosaic, and I mustn't neglect that part. The problem comes when the focus is only–or even just mostly–on ourselves. That's when we compromise our potential for connection and therefore happiness." In other words, the self is only a small part of the whole well-being pie, and if I choose to limit my scope to that small part, then I'm neglecting the potential inherent in the rest of the pie. One hundred percent of a small part is still a small part. By also focusing on others, by giving and contributing, I make the whole pie, of which I'm a part, better.

I was reminded of a quote from the book *The Power of Nice* by Linda Kaplan Thaler and Robin Koval: "The beauty of focusing on other people's concerns is that it shifts your attention away from your own worries and anxieties. And it's a lot cheaper than therapy!"

I paid Avi for the haircut, and went to pick up my kids from school.

on silence

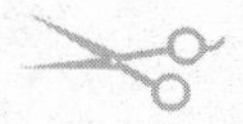

Sometimes we were silent. The sound of the scissors cutting through hair and air, the monotonous buzz of the shaver evening the field with inhuman precision, the sharp razor's crackling sound in competent, careful hands leaving smooth skin in its wake.

Much beauty resides in emptiness; much growth emerges from silence.

on selfish parenting

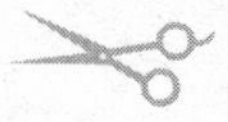

I usually went to Avi's place without a question or a topic in mind and just let the conversation unfold. This time, however, I had a clear agenda. I wanted to hear Avi's take on what I found to be the most draining part of my life: raising children. I told Avi that while my children were incredibly dear to me of course, I was often left exhausted by all the things I had to do for them: dropping them off at school, picking them up, feeding them, resolving conflicts, taking them to dance or basketball, resolving conflicts (again), bedtime routine, morning routine. "It never ends!" I concluded, and eagerly expected his response.

"Here is what I do. I demand one-on-one time with them!" He smiled.

"Demand? Are you serious?" I asked.

"Yes, totally. You see, they spend a lot of time in extracurricular activities and with friends. And at the same time they know that they have to make time for Dad."

Initially the word *demand* seemed a bit over the top to me, but when I thought about it some more, it made perfect sense—for the parent and the child. For the parent, one-on-one time with a child can be a source of much joy, which stands in contrast to the ongoing chores one has to perform as a parent; it's like the difference between hurriedly stuffing oneself with food because one has to eat, and savoring a meal bite by bite because one wants to eat. The children, beyond the enjoyment they derive from the time with their parent and the undivided attention they receive, also feel good about themselves for being a source of joy to the parent.

The Nobel Prize–winning psychologist Daniel Kahneman demonstrated in research that, compared to other activities, parents do not generally enjoy spending time with their children. One of the reasons for this is that parents are distracted by other activities or people, and when their attention is divided they find the experience strenuous and draining. In contrast, when parents spend exclusive time with their children, without conflicting demands, they are more likely to find the time they spend together enjoyable, even energizing.

Avi explained that many people think of ways to recover from the hardship of parenting by taking time off, away from the children. Adult-only time is of course important, be it for healthy parenting or for a healthy marriage, but it's equally important to make recovery an integral part of the parent-child relationship. "We do so much for our kids, and we have to remember to do for ourselves too—not just by being away from our children but also within our relationship with them."

The one-on-one times can remind us that raising children is not only a duty to be performed but also a relationship to be enjoyed. We become happier parents, as well as better parents.

A week later I was running an errand when from a distance I saw Avi, walking hand-in-hand with his daughter, both of them with wide grins on their faces.

on avi's razor

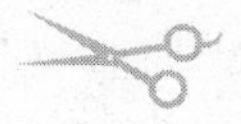

My wife, Tami, was up until this point the only person in the world who knew about the book I was writing. I didn't want Avi to find out about it before I had enough material, as I feared that it would make him self-conscious and thus take away from his ease and spontaneity. I intended to ask for his permission to publish it of course, but only after I felt that I had enough material for a short book. It was clear to me from the time I started writing that to be true to Avi, the chapters and the book as a whole would have to be short. Less is more is one of the principles he lives by, and not to honor that in this book on his principles would be inappropriate.

Avi's smile greeted me as I walked in. The noise of the hair dryer halted all conversation, but as soon as the silence returned, so did the words. The woman whose hair had been dried seemed to pick up from the point just prior to the loud intrusion: "I want to provide for my children everything that I didn't have as a child."

Avi continued styling her hair, inspecting it directly and through the mirror, shaping it with a brush and his hands. And then in a matter-of-fact manner, without a trace of judgment in his voice, he said: "I know that the intentions behind satisfying our children's every need and want are mostly good. However, beyond the bare minimum help that is absolutely necessary, the more you provide for them, the less they gain for themselves."

I immediately thought of the great educator Maria Montessori, who advised parents not to do things for children that they can do for themselves. Put differently, do for the children as little as possible and as much as necessary. If my child can tie her laces without help, then unless I'm extremely pressed for time, I have to let her do it on her own. If my child can prepare a whole meal, or a part of it, then he should prepare as much as he possibly can, with only as much help from me as absolutely necessary. That is how, over time, children become independent and confident.

Montessori's idea is a variation of a famous philosophical principle called Occam's razor. William of Occam, a fourteenth-century English philosopher, argued that in coming up with a theory, we have to make things as simple as possible and as complex as necessary. Avi's razor might then be the idea that we ought to be doing for children as little as possible and as much as necessary.

A few minutes after the exchange in the salon, Avi's razor shaved the back of my neck–leaving it as smooth as possible and without any unnecessary hair.

on lifelong learning

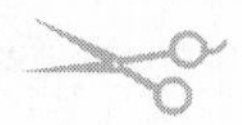

It was 6:00 PM and I was the last customer being helped. Karin had already left, so Avi shampooed my hair and then led me to the chair.

Not surprisingly, having been on his feet working for close to ten hours, Avi looked exhausted. "Long day?" I broke the silence.

"Yes"—a short reply, even from Avi.

"So is it dinner, TV, and an early night in bed?"

"Oh, no. I have to be out of here by six thirty to make it to school."

"School?"

"Yes, I started an English for Business course last month. I have my level-eleven test later this week, and I have a long way to go yet. I hope to reach level thirty by next year."

Time and again I was amazed by Avi's commitment to self-improvement and personal growth. I believe that more than anything else, the secret to his wisdom is his voracious appetite for learning. As adult-education expert Nancy Merz Nordstrom points out: "Lifelong learning enables us to . . . more fully develop the wisdom that can come with later life."

There are numerous benefits to being a lifelong learner like Avi, from improving cognitive functioning (keeping our brain alert and sharp) to bettering relationships (making us interesting and interested). Learning significantly contributes to both psychological and physical well-being, making us happier by providing us a sense of meaning in life, and making us healthier because a commitment to learning keeps us engaged with life. As an academic, I am surrounded by scholars who have dedicated their lives to learning. Unlike these professors, though, who usually specialize in a particular field using a particular research methodology, Avi sought to learn about widely different topics and from a vast range of sources, including experiences right in his own salon. Everyone and everything provided raw material for learning–from an English teacher to a client, from an experience he had to a book he read, from movies to songs.

on anger management

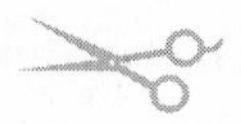

Much has been written about the Mediterranean temperament. Passionate, dramatic, impatient, intense, quick to anger and quick to love. It could be the weather, or maybe the genes, or maybe something in the water or vegetables or hummus. But whatever the cause, the effect is clear. In this part of the world, there is more honking and shouting, more hand gestures and theatrical facial expressions.

Even in the enclosed chamber of Avi's place, when the door is shut and the air conditioner is on, the outside world penetrates. The sounds enter through the cracks, and emotions often find their way in through the front door–as they did on that day. A middle-aged woman entered, sat on the sofa, and went on a rant about the rude-vulgar-foul-idiotic saleswoman she'd just met in a shoe store.

When she was done (it took a while), Avi started: "I have a very short fuse, but a technique I learned from a friend helps me control my anger." Avi went on to describe a hypothetical scenario in a parking lot. You are late for a meeting, and you've been driving around for a few minutes in search of a spot. Finally you see a person leaving the building and follow him to his car. You patiently wait for him to enter the car and drive off. But before you can move your car to claim your reward, a large SUV cuts you off and takes your spot.

"This, for me, is an invitation for a duel–or at least a driver's seat shouting match," said Avi. The woman returning from the shoe store and I nodded in agreement. Avi continued: "But I also know, not at that moment, but now when I think about it, that raising hell over that spot will only hurt me. Even if I do win the argument or fight, anger has a way of eating us from the inside."

"So what do you do?" the woman asked Avi.

"I imagine that instead of an SUV cutting me off, a cow had just cut me off."

The woman and I laughed.

"See? It works! If a cow stole your spot, you're more likely to laugh than pick a fight with her. So why not use your imagination, and then you won't have to spend the rest of the day fuming? We should learn to pick our battles better—sometimes it's appropriate and right to get angry or upset, but sometimes, usually in fact, it's just not worth it."

There is a lot of research in psychology on substituting emotions—replacing anger with empathy or stress with excitement. For example, psychologist Joe Tomaka helped students with documented test anxiety to see an exam as challenging—rather than threatening—and as a result they became calmer, more creative, and performed better. Substituting a word (threat with challenge) or an image (evil SUV with holy cow) can help us reframe a situation and experience it very differently.

My homework for the day was to come up with different images that I could prepare in advance for dealing with frustrating situations. One image I found useful was of a wise friend laughing at a cow in a parking lot.

on hurt management

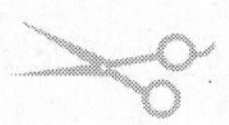

I waved to Avi through the window as I walked past his salon toward the grocer, and while he waved back I could see on his face and from his posture that all was not well. He had a client in his chair, so I decided to do my shopping first, and check in on him after. A few minutes later, he was alone, and I walked in.

"What's going on?" I asked.

"I'm a little sad," he said, smiling.

"What happened?" I probed.

"I told a customer about my business venture—you know, with the hair dye? The only thing he had to say back was that I'm at a great disadvantage because my English is not so good. It's not news to me, which is why I'm taking classes, but the way he said it . . . it hurt me."

Neither of us spoke for a couple of minutes. No voices, no scissors clinking, just the quiet hum of the air conditioner melding with the purr of a distant highway.

"When I'm hurt," Avi finally offered, "I usually first just allow myself to experience it fully. You talk about doing that, right? Giving oneself the permission to be human?"

I nodded.

He continued: "But today I did something else, something I recently started doing when someone hurts me." He smiled, looking at me. "I hugged him."

"You hugged him? Why?"

"Because he needed it. Those who hurt others usually are doing it because they themselves are hurt. They desperately need some TLC, so I give it to them."

I thought about some cruel research done on animals that I heard about once, showing that when a particular animal is hurt, by an electric shock for instance, its first instinct is to attack the animal right next to it. Pain causes animals–and humans–instinctively to lash out.

Most of the time, hurting others stems from an automatic, mindless reaction to our own hurt. And unfortunately, whether with animals or with humans, the hurt escalates, spirals up, as each side reacts to the pain inflicted on her or him. This explains interpersonal conflicts and often international conflicts–where a small disagreement or a trivial dispute spirals out of control.

I know that Avi is no pacifist, but he is also unwilling to enter conflict unless absolutely necessary. By hugging the person who inflicted hurt, what Avi chose to do was undermine the potential escalation and put an end to unnecessary hurt.

Avi believes that human nature is essentially good, and that cruel or insensitive behavior is usually a response to our own internal pains. Those who inflict pain often, more than anything else, need a warm embrace, so that they stop hurting others–and themselves.

on sharing

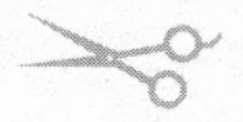

Avi's hair salon is right next to our neighborhood convenience store, so after running my errands I would sometimes drop in for a chat. As I was about to leave one such visit, one of our neighbors walked in looking frazzled and distressed. Apparently he had missed an appointment he'd made for hours earlier.

"It was an insanely busy day, I barely had time to breathe," he said. "I'll come in tomorrow, same time, OK?"

"No problem," said Avi. "Can I make you some coffee?"

"No, thank you. No time." He turned to leave.

I was expecting their conversation to end there, but Avi had other ideas.

"I'm about to have my cup of coffee. Why don't you join me? Just a few minutes, I promise."

The client paused, probably his first pause of the day, and then said, "OK sure, why not. Five minutes."

The next time I walked in for a chat, Avi reminded me of this exchange when he explained another of his famous philosophies to me, this one on coffee: "As you know, I always offer my clients coffee when they come in. But whenever possible, and always when it's necessary, I don't just give coffee, I share coffee."

I must have looked a little puzzled at his semantics, so he went on: "Some people just need to be given something, and they're satisfied. Other people, they are not open for one reason or another to receive—they may be too busy or hurt or something—but they are probably ready to share, to join in."

Roy Baumeister, a world-renowned social psychologist, wrote similarly about the need to belong—about our fundamental and innate need to form interpersonal relationships, to maintain social bonds, to be part of a shared community. Some four hundred years earlier, the English poet John

Donne pointed out, "No man is an island, entire of itself; every man is a piece of the continent, a part of the main." We want to, often need to, join in, belong.

When we share something with another–a cup of coffee, our time, our advice, our ear–it means that we're in it together. We remind those we're with, as well as ourselves, that we're not alone.

on praising effort

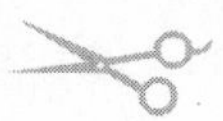

Avi's son walked into the salon as Karin was shampooing my hair, her adept hands preparing me for my monthly ritual. "Avi is such a great father," she said. "He just knows how to speak to his kids."

Waiting in the barber's chair, I could see reflected in the mirror Avi and his son talking in the corner. Avi was helping his son prepare for a geography test, and together they were listing the names of the Israeli coastal cities, starting with Ashkelon in the south. When Avi's son reached Nahariya in the north, Avi praised him: "I'm proud of you for listening so intently in class, and for putting in all the hard work for the exam." Whenever

Avi complimented his children–whether on their studies or their performance on the soccer field–he always focused on their effort and hard work rather than on how talented or successful they were: "I reward Agam for taking the journey rather than reaching the destination."

Most parents believe, as I did for many years, that telling children that they are smart or beautiful or talented is a good thing. They think it will enhance their children's self-esteem, success, and happiness. It turns out, though, that such praise hurts our kids more than it helps them.

Stanford psychologist Carol Dweck randomly assigned fifth-grade students to two groups. Students in both groups were given a number of fairly difficult, though age-appropriate, questions, and they generally answered most of the questions correctly. After completing the task, participants in the first group were praised for their intelligence (along the lines of "you're so smart"), while kids in the second group were praised for their efforts ("you worked so hard").

In the second round of the study, participants had to choose between taking a new test they were told was difficult, and from which they would learn, and one that was a lot easier. The majority of students in the first group (who'd been told how smart they were) chose the easy test. In stark contrast, 90 percent of those in the second group (praised for their efforts) chose the difficult test that offered them an opportunity to learn.

In the third round of the study, students from both groups were given a test that was objectively too difficult for their age group. Group one reported feeling miserable and frustrated while they struggled through the exam; on the other hand, group two actually enjoyed struggling and learning. As Dweck explains, "When you praise kids' intelligence and then they fail, they think they're not smart anymore, and they lose interest in their work. In contrast, kids praised for effort show no impairment and often are energized in the face of difficulty."

Interestingly, when Dweck then gave both groups one final test with the same difficulty level as the very first test they took, the "smart" students of the first group performed significantly worse than they did in the first round of the study. The "hardworking" students of the second group performed better than they did before.

Avi intuitively knew how to praise his children in a way that would teach them to embrace challenges. I wish I had such intuition, but I don't, and so I have to continue reminding myself of what I ought to do by reading research, and going for haircuts.

on talk therapy

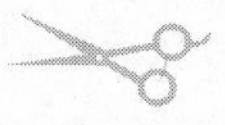

In a world where most people cannot afford the cost of therapy (money and time), barbers and hairdressers can perhaps provide a less expensive and less time-consuming substitute. While there are of course major differences between the analyst's job description and the barber's or the hairdresser's, there are also striking similarities. The professional–barber or analyst–often takes his or her position behind the client. During each session, there is no prescribed or preplanned topic of conversation; free association reigns supreme. And once a person finds his or her therapist or barber, the relationship can last for years.

While Avi did not have a beard or smoke a cigar, and despite the fact that he was of Moroccan rather than Austrian descent, his words often called to mind Freud's writings. Like Freud, Avi recognized the importance of both work and love, and many of our conversations revolved around one or both of these topics. However, while Freud lived his life with a strong emphasis on his work, often paying a price in the realm of love, Avi insisted on finding the right balance between the two.

Going in for a much-needed haircut, I found Avi's salon closed. I had forgotten it was a Tuesday—which is when he takes the afternoon off. The following day, when sitting on Avi's couch, listening to Buika's "No Habrá Nadie En El Mundo" in the background, I asked him what he had done the previous day.

"I spent it with my family, just hanging out." He then added: "If only people brought the same levels of commitment to their relationships as they do to their work, relationships would look a lot different. Their lives would be a whole lot better."

It's no big surprise that divorce levels are at an all-time high, and that most of those who have been together for more than a few years do not enjoy the kind of loving relationships they were expecting when they first tied the knot. It's no surprise that family ties are by and large becoming weaker. Avi talked about the double standards that exist in the world of work and love: "After finding their dream job, people invest huge amounts of effort trying to make it work; in contrast, when it comes to love, most people stop investing in their relationship after the honeymoon is over." The law of attraction, unlike the law of gravity, requires constant cultivation. The notion that all it takes to live happily ever after is to fall deeply in love belongs in fairy tales.

When I initially walked in for a haircut that afternoon, I was exhausted after a long day at work. But following the time I spent free-associating with Avi, I went home rejuvenated, eager to spend time with my loved ones.

on trust

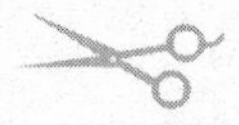

As I walked in for my monthly haircut, Avi was styling the hair of a COO of a large high-tech company who happened to live nearby. While I'd seen her before in the neighborhood, I never registered she'd be a customer of his and was a little surprised to see her there. She didn't notice me walking in; she was focusing on her hair with the same intensity, I imagined, that she brought to scrutinizing Excel sheets at work.

The COO was asking many questions, and Avi patiently responded. When she asked Avi to cut her hair a little shorter, he advised against it: "Hair has mass and is pulled down by gravity, but without enough mass it puffs up. Any shorter, and this is what would happen to your hair," he said as he formed the shape of a large puffy ball with his hands.

A few minutes later, as the COO walked out, she said, with a smile: "You know, I came in today nervous about getting this new style. But you gained my trust." Avi smiled, but it was a sad, uncharacteristic smile.

He was also uncharacteristically quiet as he decimated the mass of hair on the side of my head with a buzzer. So to make conversation, I started where the previous client left off: "How do you gain people's trust with their hair?"

"I don't know," he said with a frown. "It's funny that she talked about trust, because a couple of days ago I lost trust in a close business associate. A friend. We'd been working together for three years and he let me down."

A few minutes went by with neither of us talking. John Legend singing "All of Me" filled the emptiness. I wasn't sure if Avi was listening or thinking about his friend, but I didn't want to disturb him. However, as soon as the song was over, he said: "The best way to gain trust is to give trust."

"What happened with my friend saddens me," he continued, "but it's not going to change the way I relate to others. Giving trust is not about the other person as much as it is about the way I want to live my life, the way I want to be in the world." He was, once again, quiet for a couple of minutes, and then added: "I've been let down before, and I probably will be let down in the future, but usually my trusting others leads them to trust me."

There is much research on what psychologists call equity theory, which shows that most people have the need to reciprocate what they get from others; in fact, most of us feel discomfort when we're unable to give back something of equal value. This applies to material things, like a gift or money, as well as to nonmaterial things like kindness or trust. In other words, trust begets trust–most of the time.

And when it doesn't, Avi's advice is that, in the midst of disappointment and sadness, we need to continue to trust ourselves, our way.

on honoring thy mother

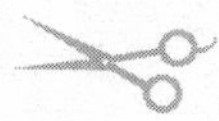

For Avi, as for most good businesspeople, the customer comes first. When the phone rings and Avi is in the middle of a haircut, he does not pick it up. When customers come in, he greets them warmly, giving them his full attention. Avi does not deviate from the "customer comes first" rule, save for one main exception. When Avi's mother calls, everything else is put on hold.

My hair was wet and Avi was about to start his magic when Karin informed him that his mother was on the line. While I couldn't hear what she was saying, I gathered from his response that she was apologizing for calling him in the middle of work. He said: "Mom, for you everything, anytime."

They spoke for a couple of minutes during which he constantly sang his mom's praises, saying things like, "You're my life," and "You're really something." And then, while she had him on the line, she figured it was a good opportunity to ask about the really important things, to which he responded: "Yes, Mom, I ate a big sandwich. I started making sandwiches for myself in the morning, when I make them for the kids."

As soon as he put the phone down, he turned around to greet a client who had walked in a minute earlier. "Hi Braha, glad to see you. Sorry for not saying hi when you walked in. The big boss called, and when she calls, I stand at attention." He smiled, and Braha, a mother herself, smiled back in maternal solidarity.

In the Bible we are commanded: "Honor thy father and thy mother: that thy days may be long upon the land which the Lord thy God giveth thee." Today, we have some scientific evidence that indirectly backs up the connection that the Bible makes between honoring our parents, or the elderly in general, and longevity.

Becca Levy of Yale School of Public Health found that those with a positive view of old age lived on average more than seven years longer than those with a negative view. One of the paths to a positive view of old age, and hence to a longer life, is through honoring one's elders–because behaving respectfully toward the elderly is both a cause and an effect of an overall positive view of aging. When we honor and respect the wisdom of older people–our parents or others–spending time listening to and learning from them, we become more appreciative of them and, by extension, of aging.

Avi's clients actually benefit from his relationship to his mother: Given the health benefits of honoring one's parents, we are likely to have him around for longer, because, for him, Mom comes first.

on being lucky

As I was settling in the barber's chair for my next haircut, Avi said, seemingly out of the blue: "I constantly receive messages from different sources helping me with difficult decisions or during challenging times." I was intrigued by this unusual remark and asked him what he meant. "If you really listen, to the radio or a random conversation in a restaurant, or really look, at billboards or bumper stickers, you'll find the help you need." And then he was quiet, allowing me time to digest what he'd said.

Like many of the best teachers I've had in life, those standing in front of a classroom and otherwise, Avi would once in a while utter a thought-provoking sentence that was not on first blush utterly clear to me. In this case, it was not until after I said good-bye to Avi and continued reflecting on his message that I was able to connect some dots of that day's teachings.

British psychologist Richard Wiseman searched for the scientific, rather than mystical, reasons for why some people are considered (by themselves and others) to be lucky. Among such people, Wiseman found unusually high levels of openness to external messages: "They are skilled at creating and noticing chance opportunities." Whereas an unlucky person may overlook or miss a relevant sentence or word on the radio, a helpful hint or suggestion on a billboard, a lucky person will stop, take note, and make the most of the message that, it seems, by chance crossed his or her path.

Along similar lines, one of the techniques that leading creativity expert Edward de Bono recommends for team problem solving is randomly choosing a word from the dictionary. People then use the word as a starting point for the discussion around the issue at hand. Every word, even the most arbitrary, holds an important message—or the potential to connect us to an important message.

While things haven't always been easy for Avi, and like most people he has his fair share of challenges, he does indeed consider himself a very lucky man. Which is another characteristic that Wiseman identified in lucky people: Believing that you're lucky is likely to make you so; expectations become a self-fulfilling prophecy.

I feel very lucky to have met Avi.

on changing

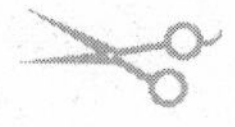

I walked into the salon and felt as if I were on the set of the beauty school dream scene (with Frankie Avalon crooning, flanked by tin-foiled Pink Ladies) from *Grease*. Three women were sitting on the sofa, two with rollers in their hair and one with foil. A fourth was center stage, sitting in the chair, with Avi styling to the rhythm of José Feliciano's "Rain" in the background.

"I'll come back later," I said, speaking over the music, feeling a little out of place, as if I had just walked in on the movie scene without knowing my lines or choreography. "Yes, this afternoon will be a lot quieter for us to talk," he said, and then added: "I want to show you something that you can think about in the meantime." He went to the front counter and handed me his smartphone. "For years, each morning, a friend of mine texts me some words to reflect on. Here's what he sent today."

> Life changes,
> and when life changes the rules change,
> and when the rules change we need to write
> a new rule book.
> Today, be mindful: Maybe your life has changed, and only you haven't?

We so often try to fit reality into our predetermined models, forgetting that our models need to be shaped by reality rather than the other way around. I thought back to all those business school case studies where managers failed because they refused to accept that the market had changed and a new approach was needed. Peter Drucker, considered the founder of modern management, noted toward the end of the twentieth century that "in a period of upheaval, such as the one we are living in, change is the norm." Not recognizing and embracing this norm is a recipe for failure, even more so today than it was only a few decades ago.

The importance of being open to change doesn't just apply to the realm of business. So many relationships flounder because one of the partners refuses to accept that the other has changed or is different from some archetype of the "perfect" partner.

Life would be a lot richer if, instead of imposing our expectations on the future or other people or the world, we were open to be "surprised by joy" and able to experience joy in the surprise. If there is no grand plan for us, or even if there is and we're not aware of it, then why hold on so tightly to our written rules? Rules are made to be rewritten.

Fortunately, at least some of the time, life unfolds according to plan, as it did later that afternoon when I had Avi's wisdom all to myself.

on the wrong foot

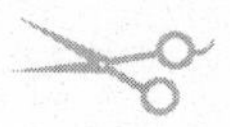

One of the challenges that I face as a positive psychologist is that people expect me to be happy all the time. Even though I wrote a book on the importance of failure and the inevitability of painful emotions, the assumption of many of my students and even close friends is that I am somehow exempt from the dark side. I have been labeled a "happiness expert" and that means that I have the answers to any and all psychological challenges. Labels stick and are often hard to remove.

What makes me really happy when I'm around Avi is that I don't have to be happy. He really sees me, hardships and all. Carl Rogers, considered the father of client-centered therapy, claimed that "empathic understanding"–the ability to simply be there for the other person–is key to the therapeutic process. So when I came in one morning, feeling (and looking) melancholy, he welcomed me with open arms, an empathic smile, and an understanding silence. I could just be, and he was just present, with me.

When he was fine-tuning my haircut–straightening the sideburns and cleaning the nape of the neck–he broke the silence: "A friend just gifted me with this most wonderful sentence: To move forward, you also need the wrong foot."

He returned to silence, and asked me to listen to the song "Je vole" by the French singer Louane Emera. When it was over, he told me that it was the theme song from the movie *La famille Bélier*, which is about the singer herself, whose parents and brother are deaf.

Why did Avi choose to prescribe this particular song and movie on this particular day? I asked him, but he wouldn't tell me. All he said was: "You'll tell me after you watch the movie. It's yours now."

I watched it, and understood. The movie is about the richness that exists in silence, the beauty of music, the value of relationships, and the pain that often accompanies us as we move forward.

on relationships

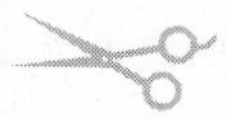

I came in early to have my haircut, as I had a busy day ahead of me, and found Avi on the phone with his mom. They spoke for a few minutes about the people who would be over the following night for dinner; then he told her that he loved her and put the phone down.

"You speak to her every day?" I asked.

"Of course," he said.

"Do you go over for dinner every Friday night?" I asked.

"Of course."

This wasn't that much of a surprise. In Israel many kids–young and old–speak to their moms daily, and many families get together on Friday nights. These regular family gatherings are my favorite part of living in Israel.

There's a lot of research in psychology that is commonsensical, predictable. For example, most people don't need a scientific study to convince them that physical exercise is good for them or that expressing gratitude for what they have can boost their levels of well-being. However, when it comes to studies that look at national levels of happiness, the results are somewhat surprising. The countries that consistently find themselves at the top of the happiness rankings include Denmark, Colombia, Costa Rica, Australia, and Israel. While not too many people find it surprising that Denmark or Australia make the cut, Israel and Colombia's presence does raise eyebrows. Both countries have had, and still have, their fair share of challenges. So why?

When researchers asked this question, they came up with a clear answer. The single common characteristic among the happiest countries in the world is that people there feel that they have strong social support–there is an emphasis on relationships; it is a priority.

I shared these findings with Avi and he said, "Of course, there is nothing, nothing more important than family and friends." While many people the world over would agree with this idea, most people in the modern world do not live in accordance with it. Relationships often take a back seat to financial or professional pursuits.

When Avi speaks to his mom every day and spends much time with her and his family, he is conveying–in words and in deeds–that relationships are a priority for him. When a client comes in and he expresses sincere interest in her well-being, or when a friend calls and Avi races to meet him and offers help, he is providing the very social support that is the DNA of happiness.

The song "In a Bar" by Tango with Lions was playing in the background. The next client came in as Avi was releasing me from the cape dusted with snips of black and white hairs that he'd just removed from my head. I said good-bye to my friend and went to work, a little happier than when I came in.

on gardening

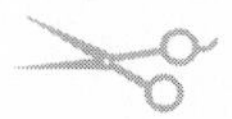

Avi would regularly use metaphors from nature when talking to his clients, as he did when he told a middle-aged woman how to let her hair grow: "If you want a petunia plant to blossom, you cannot constantly cut it down; you need to allow nature to take its course first, and only then prune it."

The ancient Greeks held up the garden as an ideal archetype for the way we ought to live our lives, for a garden embodies the unity between nature and nurture, the wild and the cultivated. According to the Greeks, an ideal human life relied on celebrating human nature and applying our human ability to nurture and improve.

As soon as the now-blossoming woman left, Avi turned to pruning me. "I was reminded of an important lesson this week," he said to me, seamlessly continuing the conversation he'd had with the previous client.

"What's the lesson?" I asked eagerly.

"That often the best way to solve problems is to do nothing." He paused, focusing on trimming my sideburns, before proceeding: "Most people, when they face a problem, become obsessed with solving it. This is sometimes good, but usually when we just do nothing and let nature take its course, problems either resolve themselves or the solution becomes apparent to us and we know exactly what we need to do."

When he finished, my mind drifted to the problem that I had been struggling with incessantly for the past week. I had received scathing feedback on a manuscript I'd submitted to my trusted editor, and since then I'd been obsessively writing and rewriting, fixing what I thought needed fixing, and yet knowing that I was making absolutely no progress. I'd reached the point where I felt my only choices were to just throw the current version away and start fresh, or to throw up my hands and delegate the project to my coauthors. But after listening to

Avi, I could see that I had another choice: I resolved to do nothing and set the manuscript aside for a while.

I reflected on how Avi's advice was backed by an abundance of research in the area of innovation—research suggesting that to find creative solutions to problems, we often need to let go, to give ourselves the time and space to venture outside the box. A gardener needs to know when to work the land and prune the flowers, and when to step back and allow nature to take its course.

When I got home, I sat by my computer and opened a Word document. I was typing not in the file of the rejected manuscript, but a fresh, new chapter in the book on the wisdom of my nurturing barber.

on dreaming

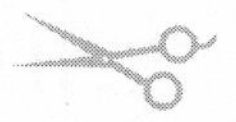

The walls of Avi's salon were painted a crisp, clean white, unadorned save for words from John Lennon's "Imagine" scrawled all around the perimeter. Avi was definitely a dreamer.

"Every morning when I wake up," he told me once, "I remind myself how fortunate I am. Think about it: Thousands of people go to sleep each night and don't wake up in the morning. They can no longer pursue their dreams. Not only that, they can no longer have dreams."

Avi was talking about two different aspects relating to dreams: pursuing dreams and having dreams–both of which are critical for a happy and fulfilling life. First of all, pursuing our dreams and actively putting ourselves on the line–as opposed to running away from our calling and avoiding the pursuit–is an essential component of healthy self-esteem and hence happiness. Second, the mere act of dreaming as a form of aspiration is an important antidote to depression and unhappiness in general. In fact, the key difference between sadness (which everyone experiences sometimes, even happiness experts and wise barbers) and depression (which some people suffer from) is hope. People who are sad can envision a remedy to their sadness, whereas those who are depressed lack hope for any kind of improvement. Dreams are the very substance of that hope.

I found it interesting, and telling, that Avi did not mention fulfilling dreams as important. It's certainly true that we are more likely to achieve something if we first imagine ourselves achieving it. However, for long-term happiness, as research by Harvard psychologist Daniel Gilbert shows, having dreams and pursuing them matters more than seeing them come to fruition.

And for that, we don't need to be extraordinarily successful or accomplished. All we need to do is wake up in the morning–and appreciate the fact that we can dream.

on golden hands and means

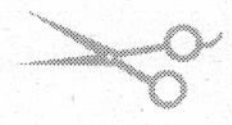

Avi is not only a great source of wisdom, he is also a great barber. His customers, myself included, refer to his golden hands–his ability to satisfy David's desire during the World Cup to look like Ronaldo, or a woman's desire before her daughter's wedding to look like Grace Kelly. Putting his phenomenal skill together with his sound business sense, Avi could have easily expanded way beyond his little salon.

So I asked him one day why he chose not to grow his business by taking a bigger place in a more central location in the city, or opening other branches. He said that he had thought about it a number of times but in the end decided against it: "I asked myself, is this something I really want, or something others think I should do?" Avi went on to explain the can-must link that's so pervasive in our culture: the belief that if you can grow, you must grow. But why?

"You see, I can only eat with one fork and one knife. I know many people for whom growing their business is appealing for all the right reasons, because they see it as a challenge or something new and fun, and that's good for them; for me, it's not." He then quoted Maimonides, the twelfth-century Jewish sage: "There is no man who dies having attained half of his desires."

Avi explained that over a decade ago he understood that no matter how much he had—a bigger house, a faster car, a fatter bank account—he would always want more. He could choose to continue in the rat race and never satisfy his desires, or to stop the race and be satisfied with what he had. He went on to quote another Jewish source, the *Chapters of the Fathers*: "Who is rich? He who is happy with his lot."

Avi paused. "I'm not saying that I want to go back to having nothing, to struggle financially like when I was growing up or just starting out. I'm glad that I'm doing well. When I was a child in Jaffa, we had a saying: 'If you have a lot of money, you have problems; if you are poor, you have troubles.' I don't want to be poor, and at the same time, I certainly don't need to be rich."

This insight from Avi's childhood, which guided him throughout his life, was the same insight that Aristotle based his entire moral theory on. According to Aristotle, who greatly influenced Maimonides, we ought to strive for the golden mean–the middle path between excess and deficiency, between too much and too little.

Enrique Iglesias was singing "Bailando" in the background. Avi was humming the melody as he cut my hair. All was good.

on slowing down

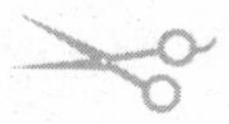

Avi always encouraged his customers to slow down. "Why the hurry?" he would ask them as they poked their head in, saw that there were other heads waiting, and said that they would come later. "Bring yourself in, sit with us."

This statement always reminded me of Buddhists, who often refer to meditation as a "sitting session." And indeed the sense of calm I felt after sitting with Avi was in many ways similar to what I felt after meditating or practicing yoga.

Observing some of the clients heed Avi's call to come inside made me think that hair salons could provide the fertile soil from which a countercultural revolution could grow. Right now our culture is addicted to speed, looking for fast food and fast cars, quick fixes and quick sex, immediate gratification and immediate impact. The unit of measuring time has become the nanosecond, and long-term success is determined by quarterly earnings. And yet with the exponential increase in speed, more and more people are left behind, unhappy and unfulfilled. Most hair salons today provide the antidote to speed. Waiting your turn, washing, cutting, trimming, washing again, waiting some more before straightening or curling–these all take time. And while there are those who find the time getting their hair cut painful because they could have been elsewhere getting ahead, many others find the experience relaxing and replenishing–finding themselves on an island of sanity, surrounded by friendly people and no place to run.

Carl Honoré in his book *In Praise of Slowness* points to the value of taking our time to make food, to make love, to make conversation. One of my most beloved teachers, the late Harvard psychologist Philip Stone, would often make the distinction between being and doing, arguing that our mostly Western obsession with doing prevents us from enjoying the fruits of being. Looking back farther, we see the nineteenth-century British author Mary Ann Evans reminding us to slow down: "The golden moments in the stream of life rush past us, and we see nothing but sand; the angels come to visit us, and we only know them when they are gone."

We are losing our capacity to stop and wait and be patient, and need to bolster this capacity by exercising it more often. And just as we go to the gym to strengthen our physical muscles, so we can go to our hair salon to strengthen our slowness muscles, so that we can savor more, experience more of the beauty that lies within and without.

on authenticity

I noticed that Avi hadn't been in for a few days, so I walked into his salon and asked Karin where he was. She told me that he was on business in Italy and Holland, and would be back next week. I thanked her and made an appointment for a couple of days after his scheduled return.

"How is the business going? Was your trip worthwhile?" I asked him when we met next.

"Very well. This morning I had a meeting with potential investors." The investors, it turned out, were the biggest players in the Israeli hair products market.

"And how did the meeting go?"

"Great!" said Avi. "They are interested in a joint venture."

"Did you enjoy the meeting?" I asked, trying to picture Avi in a very different setting from the one I usually see him in.

"I did, very much, and yet during the meeting I was thinking about how much I love my work here, more than anything else that I do in my professional life. . . . It keeps me grounded."

"What do you mean?" I asked.

"For example, my meeting earlier today was with highly accomplished senior managers, in an enormous and lavish office on the forty-fifth floor. An hour later, I found myself back here, in this little salon on the ground floor, cutting the hair of an eight-year-old. I loved it."

I asked Avi to explain what he loved about the contrast.

"It's easy to fall in the role trap, where one allows a situation to define who one is. And it's important to remember who one is regardless of the situation. It's important to be true to yourself, to be authentic."

As he spoke, I thought about the song "Runnin' (Lose It All)" by Naughty Boy and Beyoncé, which I first heard in this salon. The singers harmonize on the parallels between being ready for whatever comes our way and the risks of letting go of our true motives in life—of our true selves.

Being authentic and real, as opposed to losing oneself, is especially significant in the realm of leadership. Harvard Business School professor Bill George, himself among the most celebrated business leaders of the twentieth century, identifies authenticity as the key trait of our most effective and revered leaders. And while Avi is not world-renowned and ostensibly did not achieve what the great leaders did, he shares the quality of authenticity with the best of them.

The great leaders surely adapt to different situations and tailor their style or approach depending on who is in front of them; however, at the core, they are true to themselves. While Avi certainly spoke differently to seasoned investors than he did to a young boy, the kind, humble, and honest core remained the same.

Beyond Avi's professionalism, it's his authenticity that makes him the number-one choice of barber for eight-year-olds and forty-five-year-olds alike.

on taking a break

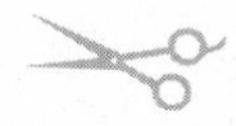

Mornings were my favorite time of day to get a haircut. There were always fewer people and more one-on-one time. On a cold wintery morning in January of 2016, Avi greeted me, as he often did, with his song du jour, the one that, in his words, would "take me places." This one was by the Israeli singer Idan Raichel, with a call to action to embrace every opportunity of every day–since who knows when we'll run out of chances?

Avi told me that he had decided to not let any more chances go by; he wanted to take a break to spend more time reading, listening to music, and visiting new places. Periodically, Avi would close shop for a week or a month, and head off on a journey. He knew that this practice wasn't great for business, and that beyond the fact that he wasn't earning any money while away, some customers might leave. He also knew, though, that there were more important things than business.

Avi often asked himself the question, "If I had one week to live, what would I do?" I have been asked this question many times before–in self-help seminars and such–but coming from Avi, it seemed to carry more weight. I knew him well enough to recognize that, for him, the question wasn't merely academic; he was living the answer.

I recently read Stanford psychiatrist Irvin D. Yalom's novel *The Schopenhauer Cure*, about a psychotherapist who has to deal with his own mortality after he's told that he has less than a year to live. Avi's reflections reminded me very much of Yalom's. Avi spoke about how, no matter if we have a week or fifty years of life ahead of us, life always feels too short for what we want to do, and, at some point, it ends. So why wait? "Moreover," he added, "even if I do live to be a hundred, I don't want to visit the Wall of China and be carried by a golf cart; I want to run up the stairs."

There is a Buddhist practice that I always thought was extreme, though interesting, which involves meditating in a cemetery. The purpose of this practice is to focus attention on the temporary nature of reality, and hence on what truly matters in the present. I doubt that Avi ever had a sitting session among the graves; he didn't need the dead to remind him to live.

"See you in a few days; I'm off to London tomorrow," I said and thanked him. He smiled and reminded me: "Have a wonderful journey."

on words

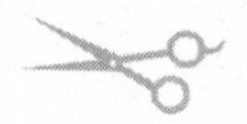

One of my sacred rituals is to have a haircut before a big lecture or before filming something. It was an unusually warm winter day, and I showed up at 9:00 AM sharp, an hour before I had to be in the studio for a HappierTV filming session. As I sat in Avi's chair going over the script in my mind, Avi noticed that I needed some quiet and did not interrupt. Shlomo Artzi filled the space with lyrics of seduction uttered by the lover of his friend, who did not return from the war; and then Nouvelle Vague took over, singing about silence and words, and everything and nothing.

A few songs later, Avi was done with me. I paid him and was about to leave when my eye caught a business card on the counter with a quote by Rabbi

Abraham Kook, one of the great Jewish scholars of the twentieth century. I picked it up and read: "The foundation of happiness is the love of truth in the mind, the love of honesty in life, the love of beauty in emotions, the love of good in deeds." Printed on the other side was the name Avi Peretz with a phone number underneath.

"Nice quote," I said. "May I take one?"

"Sure. I just had these made last week. Here's another business card, my old one, with a great quote, too." He handed the card to me as if it were a sacred scroll. On it was a quote attributed to the Dalai Lama: "Man sacrifices his health to make money, then he sacrifices his money to regain his health. He is so worried about his future that he doesn't enjoy his present. Consequently, he doesn't live in the present or the future. He lives as if he will never die, and dies as if he had never lived."

Avi didn't miss an opportunity to spread wisdom–his own or others'–through words, even when I or another client was in no mood to talk. I thanked Avi as I walked out, and he responded in the way he often responds to his clients: "With love."

on failing safely

As a social psychologist, a question that I often ask is: What makes a certain environment conducive to learning and growing? In other words, what is it about a particular social setting that brings out the best in people? This was a question that I had asked many times about Avi's place. Clearly there was something else, beyond Avi's insightful comments, that helped me and many others leave the salon not just a whole lot tidier but also a little wiser. As he often does, Avi provided me an answer through a personal story, this time about his son, Agam.

Avi told me that Agam had just gone through a tough week at school; he performed poorly on a test and was criticized by a teacher. "He was quite distressed when he came home, so I let him vent a little, and then asked him a simple question. I asked him whether he knew more now than he did before going through the tough week. He nodded and I said, 'Isn't it great, then?' His frown immediately turned to a smile."

One of the mantras I repeat over and over again–to myself, my students, and my clients–is "learn to fail or fail to learn." Failures, mistakes, and disappointments are an inevitable part of learning–and embracing failure is indispensable to both success and happiness.

Recognizing the value of learning from failure to organizational success, Harvard professor Amy C. Edmondson studies psychological safety, defining it as "a shared belief held by members of a team that the team is safe for interpersonal risk-taking." A psychologically safe environment encourages openness, self-disclosure, and mutual learning from failure. And as Avi was talking about his response to his son's experience, it dawned on me that this was precisely the kind of environment that he masterfully created–whether for his kids, or for his clients. When it's safe, really safe, to be vulnerable and go through tough times, then instead of running away from failure and criticism, we run toward learning and growing. A psychologically safe environment can turn fear of failure into love of learning, a broken self into a self on a quest, a frown into a smile.

I walked out of Avi's safe place inspired once again, thinking about how it was possible to recreate the kind of environment that Avi had created—to provide my kids at home, my students in class, and my colleagues at work an environment where it was OK to make mistakes, to fail, and to joyfully learn from it all.

on divine connection

The range of conversations that Avi's salon entertained each day never ceased to amaze me. Each person–whether a client or a visitor–brought his or her topic, and Avi would go along, providing his witty commentary or his wise silence. As I walked in one afternoon, the conversation revolved around the renovation happening at the neighborhood synagogue.

The rabbi, I learned, was trying to attract more people to services. An elderly gentleman who was not having a haircut, but came in anyway to spend some time on Avi's couch, commented on how difficult it was to attract the younger generation to attend the synagogue. He talked about how the virtual was replacing the real, adding that "even the religious ones are just downloading an app to pray!" He turned to Avi, looking at him through the mirror: "I actually just downloaded one myself, and it's quite good. Do you want me to download it for you?"

In response, Avi put down his scissors and signaled to the gentleman to follow him. They walked outside the glass door, and Avi pointed to the heavens: "I don't need an app to pray, nor any other intermediaries. I have a direct connection."

I was reminded of Ralph Waldo Emerson, who back in 1838 addressed the graduating class of the Harvard Divinity School. It was the speech that got Emerson banished from the church because he claimed that we didn't need intermediaries to converse with God, that we had direct access to the divine.

Avi was always direct, in his speech and in his experience of life. He was disturbed by the fact that kids spent hours upon hours each day playing video games rather than playing in the sandbox, that for most people watching a high-speed chase on TV replaced observing the sun as it slowly set over the sea, and that friends interacted through

Facebook rather than face-to-face. He was a staunch advocate of less technology and more reality, and sought direct connection to other people, to the earth, and to God.

It was a bright day, and on my walk home I noticed the sound of the birds conversing with passion, the leaves beginning to appear on the trees, and the vast blue sky above. I felt divine.

on paying it forward

As I mentioned at the beginning of this book, one of the reasons I chose to write about Avi was to share his wisdom with those who do not have the good fortune of being his clients–or, as I like to think of myself and my neighbors, his students. And while Avi had no idea that I had been writing about him for almost two years and had not yet agreed to my publishing his words, I was confident that he would give his consent. He is all about paying it forward.

Recently, a teenage girl walked into the salon and asked Avi to fund the printing of thirty-two shirts she was making for her camp. In return, she said, Avi could advertise his business on the shirts. Avi agreed to help her, on two conditions.

First, instead of the name of his business on the shirt, he asked her to print a picture of a funny face–one that would make people laugh. Second, each camper who received the shirt had to pay for it by performing an anonymous act of kindness for somebody else.

The impact of Avi's generosity rippled out of the salon, reaching far and wide. Whenever people smiled or laughed looking at the funny picture on the shirt, their body released chemicals that actually made them feel better. By asking the girls to commit an act of kindness, Avi was not only spreading goodness, he was also disseminating happiness and health. Psychologist Sonja Lyubomirsky demonstrated in her research that giving increases our own levels of psychological as well as physical well-being.

The movie *Pay It Forward* highlights the exponential nature of human interactions, and potentially of human generosity. A young boy, played by Haley Joel Osment, devises a plan to change the world for the better by performing three generous acts and asking the recipients of these acts to do so themselves for three other people, initiating that ripple effect. A simple calculation shows that if each person receiving help in turn helped three others, within twenty-one steps every person in the world would receive help.

The nice thing about generosity is that we are more likely to be kind to others if someone was just kind to us. Generosity is highly contagious. So is Avi's wisdom.

on gifts, great and small

It was March 14, 2016. Exactly two years had passed since I'd started writing this book, and a few months earlier I had decided that today would be the day when I would tell Avi about the book and ask for his permission to publish it. After all, it was more his book than mine.

So, at around 10:00 AM, I called him up. "How are you?" I asked.

"Very good, plus," was his response.

"Can I come in and see you?"

"Of course. Anytime."

We decided to meet at noon, and as soon as I put the phone down I raced to my computer and printed the manuscript I'd completed a week before.

Walking toward the salon, I saw him sitting outside, his bronze-colored skin absorbing the sun, his muscular arm resting on a table that seemed to be supported by his arm rather than supporting it. The feeling of excitement that I usually had as I approached his salon was replaced with nervous anxiety. What if he didn't like what I wrote? What if he said no? What if this changed everything between us, and I needed to find a new barber, and teacher?

He greeted me with his usual smile–the genuine, simple smile I so cherished and desperately didn't want to change. My lips and tongue felt swollen and dry as I tried to smile back; my voice trembled as I asked him how he was doing. I sat down and rested my hand awkwardly on the table.

"What is it, friend?" he asked, noticing my discomfort.

I went right to it, having rehearsed what I was going to say countless times: "Exactly two years ago today, I decided to write a book about the words you shared with me and with others, the words that have helped me and made a difference in my life."

I stopped, and he was quiet, the smile gone. I couldn't quite make out his expression, so I continued. I told him about how each time I came over, something he said or did would resonate, and I would briefly write about it when I got home. I then took out the manuscript from my bag, handed it to him, and said that I would love to publish it for others to read–but only if he agreed.

The manuscript in his hand seemed light, the wind blowing the corners of the pages, as his eyes inspected its content. A few seconds passed, and he looked up, saying, "Wow, that's amazing, I can't wait to read it. I'm leaving for Italy tomorrow, and will take it with me on the trip."

Another client was waiting in the salon, and Avi got up to attend to him. He smiled at me, his usual smile returned, and embraced me firmly, squeezing out the remaining drops of anxiety.

On his way to the airport the following day, Avi sent me a WhatsApp message, thanking me for the book, which he described as a "great gift." I wrote back that, for a change, I'd like to ask him to listen to the words of a song by Israeli singer Rami Kleinstein, one that describes the "little gifts" that pass from generation to generation–feelings and thoughts, melodies and memories–that together help us find some calm and acceptance amid life's inevitable storms and concerns.

The chorus ends with the words: "What more can one ask for?"

ACKNOWLEDGMENTS

It always takes a village to write a book, and this book is a product of my neighborhood—my warm and loving village—in Ramat Hasharon.

Special thanks to Yuval and Shani Kutz, my dear friends and partners, for invaluable comments and support in writing this book, and in my life.

I am grateful to Jennifer Kurdyla, my brilliant and insightful editor at The Experiment, who gets me and elevates me. Thank you to Matthew Lore and Jennifer Hergenroeder of The Experiment for believing in this unconventional book, and for providing me a publishing home. Thank you to Rafe Sagalyn and Brandon Coward of the Sagalyn agency, for over a decade of working and playing together.

To my three kids, David, Shirelle, and Eliav, who had their hair cut a little more often than necessary during the two years of writing this book. And for being the light of my life.

To my parents, my role models, who taught me to learn and to listen; to Zevik, Ateret, Udi, and Dyonna, to Guy, Alon, and Lavi–I'm blessed.

Finally, to Tami, the only person in the world who knew I was writing this book as I was writing it. You are my most trusted and best friend.

ABOUT THE AUTHOR

TAL BEN-SHAHAR, PHD, taught the largest course at Harvard, "Positive Psychology," and the third-largest, "The Psychology of Leadership," attracting 1,400 students per semester–approximately 20 percent of all Harvard undergraduates. Ben-Shahar obtained his BA and PhD from Harvard, and for the last fifteen years has been teaching leadership, happiness, and mindfulness to audiences all over the world. He is the author of five previous books, including *Choose the Life You Want* and the international bestsellers *Happier* and *Being Happy*, which have been translated into more than twenty-five languages.